THREE-DIMENSIONAL DECOUPAGE

THREE-DIMENSIONAL DECOUPAGE

Letty Oates

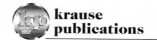 krause
publications

A QUARTO BOOK

 **krause publications**

700 E. State Street • Iola, WI 54990-0001
Telephone: 715/445-2214

Please call or write for our free catalog of publications. Our toll-free number to
place an order or obtain a free catalog is 800-258-0929 or please use our regular business
telephone 715-445-2214 for editorial comment and further information.

This book was designed and produced by
Quarto Publishing plc
The Old Brewery
6 Blundell Street
London N7 9BH

Senior art editors Catherine Shearman, Julie Francis
Designer Neville Graham
Project editor Anne Hildyard
Managing editor Sally MacEachern
Editor Mary Green
Photographer Jon Bouchier
Picture researcher Miriam Hyman
Art director Moira Clinch
Editorial director Pippa Rubinstein
Project maker Labeena Ishaque
Chapter openers made by Mary Fellows

Typeset in Great Britain by
Type Technique, London W1
Manufactured in Singapore by United Graphics (Pte) Ltd
Printed in Singapore by
Star Standard Industries (Pte) Ltd

CONTENTS

INTRODUCTION

Decoupage is the art of decorating surfaces with applied paper cutouts. The word decoupage comes from the French *decouper*, which means to "cut out". Motifs are cut from paper and then glued flat onto a surface and heavily varnished so that the edges blend in with the background, almost as if the motif was painted onto the surface. One of the primary goals is to get the motifs as smooth and flat as possible.

The term "three-dimensional decoupage," then, seems to be a contradiction in terms, since the paper motifs are freestanding and not a part of the surface as they are in traditional decoupage. Unlike two-dimensional decoupage, three-dimensional decoupage gives an effect of depth and volume – in effect a "trompe l'oeil," a trick of the eye. The composition looks almost lifelike, and has a richness and realism that a flat design would find it impossible to compete with. Three-dimensional designer Sheila Sawyer calls the craft "elevated decoupage."

There are differing opinions on the history of decoupage. Some sources say that it is an early European art, dating from the twelfth and thirteenth centuries, which became popular in seventeenth century Venice and then spread throughout Europe. Others say that it began in fifteenth century Germany, when printed decorative borders simulating the complex Tarsia wood inlay were produced for use on furniture, so that from a distance it looked real. Whichever is correct, decoupage remains popular today.

However, many authors on the subject remain convinced that it

Buttons, beads, scraps of fabric and tiny cloth dolls decorate these small notebooks.

This attractive painted box is embellished with colorful beads and felt scraps.

was the demand for heavily lacquered Chinese furniture, or Chinoiserie, that began the trend towards decoupage during the late seventeenth century. This furniture was very much sought after but prohibitively expensive, meaning that few people could afford to buy it. In response to this, the Venetian craftsmen of the time decided to use decoupage to emulate the handpainted and highly lacquered effects of Chinoiserie, thereby creating a more accessible and affordable version. The craftsmen created their own designs that they painted, cut out and pasted onto items of furniture, which were then varnished heavily.

Decoupage arrived in England a little later, when people who returned from their tours of Europe took the love of decoupage with them.

Dried leaves, in autumn hues, transform a simple brown cardboard box.

This richly decorated box is covered with pearls, gold buttons and a spoon.

This delightful cherub box is adorned with satin roses, doily scraps and gold charms.

This pretty frame is bordered with pearls, ribbon and paper flowers.

The decoupage techniques used here produce a realistic picture of goldfinches.

The Victorians seemed to have an unbridled passion for this delicate art, decorating everything from boxes to screens, tables, chairs and vases. With the coming of the industrial revolution and the development of color printing, soon prints or "scrap sheets" were being produced to use specifically for decoupage purposes.

In the years since, decoupage has gone in and out of fashion, but the craft itself has remained essentially unchanged. It has experienced a resurgence in popularity over the last few years, due in part to the availability of photocopiers and fast-drying varnishes, and in part to the realization that it is such an easy way to be creative, even if you can't draw or paint. The main tool is a pair of scissors and all you have to do is cut out and paste, for which you need more enthusiasm than talent.

In contrast to traditional decoupage, three-dimensional decoupage has no long, rich history. As a craft, it has some of its origins in paper tole and collage. It is essentially an exciting and innovative extension of traditional decoupage, one that has no rules and is limited only by one's own imagination.

Having written books on decoupage previously, I was intrigued by the prospect of writing a book on three-dimensional decoupage. After spending so much time on perfecting the truly flat and heavily varnished furniture surfaces, I had to rethink my position about creating three-dimensional motifs on household items such as fireplace screens, boxes and photograph albums.

Throwing myself in at the deep end, I not only used paper

Pansies make a good subject for a three-dimensional effect.

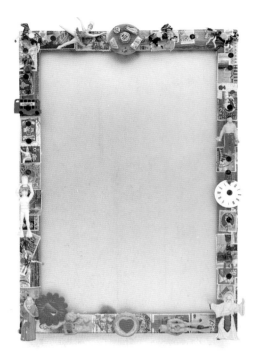

This unusual mirror has a border of stamps and miniature items.

Cut-out shapes of birds and fish adorn this "faux" cupboard picture.

motifs that had been contoured and overlaid but I also discovered uses for old scraps of lace and ribbon. Beads, dimensional paint, ribbons, rosebuds, doilies, buttons and miniature metallic die-stamped shapes have all been used to embellish the "traditional" decoupage motifs and create beautiful designs. They add to the depth and richness of the elevated decoupage, at times becoming a focal point and at other times simply framing a picture or highlighting sections of the work.

As much of the traditional decoupage took place on furniture, I too have embellished and decoupaged on objects and accessories for the home. Included are boxes, shelves, stationery, clocks and even a summer bonnet. For best results, the scale of objects used with three-dimensional decoupage should be kept smaller rather than larger, as the details get lost on a larger surface. The largest item I tackled was the fireplace screen, and only because I had the cat motifs, which fit the shape after I enlarged them on a photocopier.

The projects in this book are just a sampling of the variety of effects that one can achieve with three-dimensional decoupage. They are meant to inspire and encourage you to try some ideas of your own.

This elaborately decorated plaque has an intricate edging of leaves.

Cut-out paper scraps, net and silver ribbon are used for table adornments.

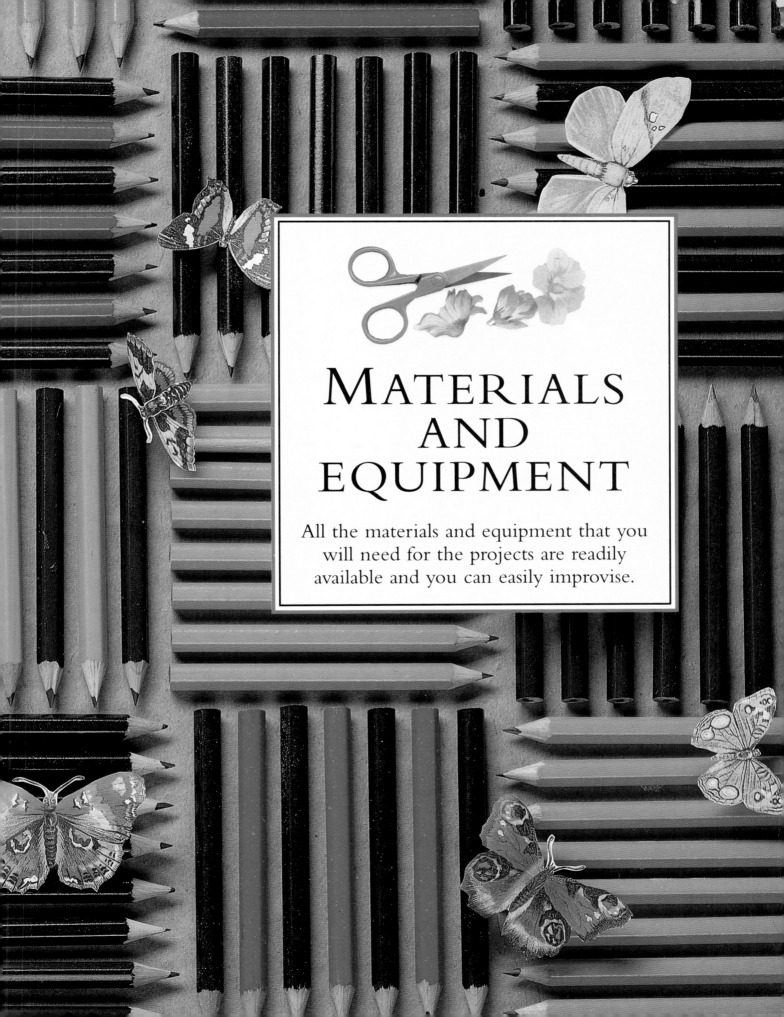

MATERIALS AND EQUIPMENT

All the materials and equipment that you will need for the projects are readily available and you can easily improvise.

TOOLS AND EQUIPMENT

One needs only a few basic materials to use in decoupage, and many of you will have most of these things at home already. The most basic equipment involves only a pair of scissors and glue. However, I have compiled a list of all the tools and equipment that you may possibly need when creating your three-dimensional decoupage masterpieces.

SCISSORS

You will need two pairs of scissors: one larger pair for cutting away surplus paper and on larger motifs, and a smaller, finer pair like manicure or embroidery scissors to do most of the cutting. Keep the scissors sharp and use them only for paper, otherwise they tend to blunt. Pinking shears are useful to make zigzag edges.

CRAFT KNIFE AND SELF-HEALING CUTTING MAT

A craft knife is a good accompaniment to the scissors, as it can be used for those tiny and intricate details. Always be very careful when using knives. Never cut towards yourself and always cut on a suitable surface. If you do not have a self-healing cutting mat, use a small sheet of glass or hardboard, so that you do not spoil the work surface beneath.

PVA OR WHITE GLUE

This glue is quick drying and can be painted onto the paper. It will stick fast and only takes fifteen to twenty minutes to dry thoroughly. When applied it goes on white, but then dries transparent. This glue is used for gluing down the entire base layer of decoupage and can also be used to adhere beads, sequins and charms to a flat surface.

SILICONE RUBBER GLUE

This glue is very similar to the silicone rubber sealant that is used in bathrooms, around showers and baths. When a blob of glue is applied to the surface and a motif laid onto it, the glue will not run, spread or shrink. It will dry holding the motif to the background, while at the same time keeping it a little distance away, to give it height. The glue is ideal for adding the top, three-dimensional layers to the base layer.

FOAM TAPE

Foam tape is available from stationery stores. It's sold in rolls in a choice of widths, and as small rectangular-shaped pads, which are adhesive on both sides. This makes it a good alternative to silicone rubber glue, as it can be cut down to size and layered to create varying heights.

   The advantage over silicone rubber glue is that there is no mess, which is often the case when using glues.

FABRIC GLUE

This is needed when gluing ribbons, lace and threads into place. Fabric will stick immediately and dry within minutes. If too much glue is applied when sticking thread to a surface (see Charming Jewelry Chest page 100), simply peel away the excess without taking off the base layer.

PAINTS

If you choose to paint the item that you want to decoupage, choose a paint that will complement the motifs and the item. Generally speaking, acrylic paint is suitable for most of the items that we have decorated in this book. Acrylic can be watered down and used as a wash or it can be applied straight from the tube to give a thick opaque coat. Latex paint is also fine for smaller wooden pieces of furniture that will be varnished after being decoupaged. In some instances spray paint is a quick and simple solution for a quick transformation. In several projects spray paints have been used to color white paper doilies.

BRUSHES

Brushes are needed in various sizes for various purposes. Use fine artists' brushes for applying PVA or white glue onto intricate motifs and for painting in details, a medium-sized brush for applying glue to larger areas, and a large decorators brush for painting surfaces prior to decoupage. When using fabric glue, use the brush provided with the glue or an old fine paintbrush, as this glue tends to spoil brushes. Always wash brushes immediately after using. In fact always keep a jar of water nearby when using brushes, so that they can be rinsed straight away.

VARNISHES

There is a huge range of varnishes to choose from, although in this book and for the purpose of three-dimensional decoupage I have used only one type of varnish, that is an acrylic varnish, which is available as gloss or matte.

TWEEZERS

Tweezers are useful for picking up small and delicate motifs, and they can be used to arrange them into place, if our fingers seem too clumsy. Tweezers are especially useful when picking up and placing small sequins and beads.

RULER, PENCILS, MARKERS, TRANSPARENT TAPE

These pieces of equipment are used occasionally and it is good to have them at hand if they are needed.

MATERIALS AND TECHNIQUES

There is an abundance of material that can be used for three-dimensional decoupage. As well as magazines, greeting cards and wrapping paper, consider using art papers, stamps or candy papers. The techniques used are simple and are described below and in the projects.

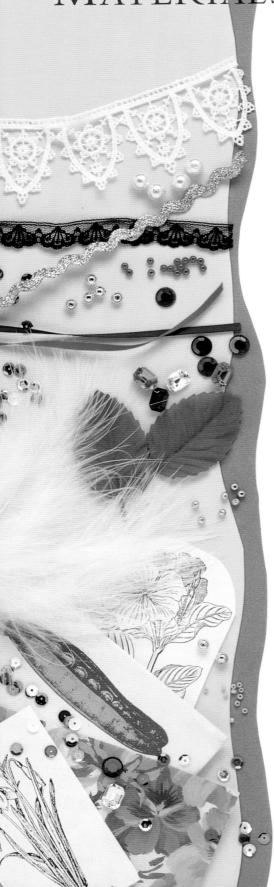

PLANNING A DESIGN

Although there are often many elements in a 3D decoupaged object, it is important that the composition of all the different parts work together. When working on a design which uses only paper motifs, one has to decide which parts of the image will stand out in relief against the background. Flowers are a popular subject for 3D decoupage and a good subject to start with. Taking at least two identical copies of a floral print, cut out the separate petals and then fit them back together again, like a jigsaw. The identical partners of these petals are then overlaid to create a three-dimensional effect.

Working with other elements apart from paper, like beads, cords, charms and three-dimensional paint, leads to a slightly different composition as these things can be added to frame a particular motif or to accentuate points on the paper motifs.

There is no set way in which to plan a design, in fact, the best way to do this is to first choose a suitable print or copy and then just experiment with the arrangement until you are happy with the composition.

SOURCING AND SELECTING MOTIFS

There are many possible sources for decoupage motifs, from prints of Old Masters to trendy wrapping papers. Search out old prints and books in second-hand book shops, thrift stores and libraries.

Use a color photocopier to copy these images and experiment with sizes and density of the colors. Although color copying can be quite expensive, it is preferable to cutting up old books, especially if they have been borrowed from the library!

Wrapping papers are a great source for decoupage; they range from traditional flowers and fruits and classical images to modern abstract designs and motifs. A sheet of wrapping paper is usually sold in a 23 × 16½ inches (60 × 40 cm) sheet. This size should be large enough to use on quite a large object, if the motifs are repeated on the sheet; otherwise it is recommended that you buy two sheets. And wrapping paper, apart from offering an enormous choice, is expensive too.

Old postcards and greeting cards are also fine to use. If the cards are too thick, simply peel off the backing card. To do this, dampen the card at the back with a wipe of a wet sponge, then slip a sharp craft knife along the card, carefully pulling the back away.

One can use prints, cards and papers of all kind on personal items, as long as you aren't planning to sell them, as the images are usually copyrighted. Some illustrated books are available to be used specifically for these purposes, and can be used without any copyrighting problems. In fact, one can even buy scraps which have been produced for decoupage purposes, although these are mainly traditional motifs like flowers, birds and various Victoriana.

In addition to the paper options for decoupage there are lots of other items that can be used to create three-dimensional effects. Paper doilies, either sprayed with metallic paints or stained with tea to give an aged look, are a perfect foil for paper motifs, and individual parts of the doilies can be cut away and used to frame pictures or they can be built up. Beads, sequins, buttons and fabric flowers are all good to use as embellishments, as are ribbons, cords and decorative threads.

Use small, sharp scissors to cut out intricate flower scraps.

CUTTING OUT MOTIFS

Before you begin to cut out the motifs, take a moment to examine the picture and consider the parts which will be the farthest away and which will be the nearest, in relation to how you will build up the picture. The number of identical copies of the image will determine the layers of your final picture

Throughout this book two pairs of scissors were used. A pair of medium scissors were used for cutting around motifs and for larger areas while a pair of manicure or embroidery scissors are perfect for cutting around more detailed and intricate motifs. If you are using small scissors keep them only for cutting paper, as they can become blunt very quickly if they are used for cutting other things and will tend to tear the paper.

Keep a craft knife with a self-healing cutting mat for the tiny and complicated motifs; a knife is ideal for cutting out the insides and centers of motifs.

CONTOURING

When you look at your chosen motif, you will notice that the two-dimensional picture will have a degree of perspective; however, gentle shaping will give it more realism.

It is important to remember that when you do contour parts of the motif, the piece will look smaller than its identical base motif, which will lie below it. Obviously, the contoured elements of your motifs will be the second layer of decoupage. The base layer should be glued down flat on to the item; this will then be covered by the contoured pieces. A flat surface helps to support the adhesives.

Pleating paper fans gives a three-dimensional effect.

The easiest and best way to contour motifs is by simply curling over edges with your fingers. Roll things like leaves and petals into a tube and then flatten them out. Glue them down only at certain points so that the edges can curl up and stand above the background.

To emphasise creases and folds (see Fanfare Photograph Album page 90), fold the lines sharply against the edge of a metal ruler, and run your thumb along the creases to make them sharp.

LAYING THE BASE PRINT

There are two ways in which to lay down the base print onto its chosen surface; either glue the back of the paper motif before arranging it into position, or glue the actual surface and then lay the motif down onto it.

Smooth over the glued motifs using your fingers or a soft cloth. If any air bubbles appear, simply pop them with a pin and push the air out of the hole. Once the motif is stuck down, check that all the edges adhere to the surface. If not, then apply a tiny amount of glue around the edges and wipe away any excess while it is still wet.

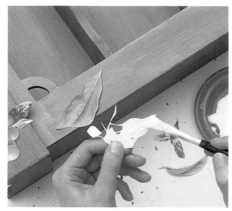

Using both glue and foam tape adds depth and dimension.

Curl up the edges of flower for a realistic effect.

Glue down any large scraps first, smoothing away any air bubbles.

Spray acrylic varnish is quick and easy to use.

GLUING

Apart from PVA or white glue, which is the ideal substance to make the base layer adhere to the surface, foam tape and silicone rubber glue are good adhesives to use in creating a three-dimensional effect with the top layers of decoupage. Both of these adhesives accentuate the depth and hold the different layers away from each other, and from the background.

Pieces of foam tape can be layered on top of each other to give varying heights to the top motif. They can also be cut down to size. Their added advantage is that they are easier to handle and less messy than glue, and they do not need any drying time, as they stick immediately.

Silicone rubber glue is actually a sealant designed to be used in bathrooms along baths and sinks; it doesn't run or shrink. It can be found in hardware stores and home improvement centers. A blob of glue can be applied to a surface straight from the tube nozzle. The blob will not spread and will keep its height. Simply lay the motif onto the glue while the glue is still wet; do not press it down. The motif will stick, although the glue will keep the motif away from the background. When using the glue it is important to use the right amount; too little will not give any height and too much will make it look as if it's floating around in midair. A wooden cocktail stick is good for applying glue to tiny areas without it spreading, and it can also be used for nudging the motif into position. Silicone rubber glue takes about an hour to dry solid and to an almost transparent, milky color.

There is no set rule on which parts to glue first, the surface or the motif. With foam tape I find it easier to attach it to the back of the motif, whereas with the silicone rubber glue it is less messy to apply the glue to the surface or base layer.

LAYERING AND BUILDING UP A PICTURE

Once the base motifs have been glued down securely onto the surface of your chosen item, begin to build up the picture. For smaller paper motifs, use tweezers to pick up and position them. Place the pieces in reverse order of appearance. In other words, the elements that are at the back should be glued down first and the "nearest" should be glued down last.

Add other embellishments at this point. In fact, items like ribbons and lace can be added between layers of paper motifs (see the Angel Mementoes Box, page 84). Beads and sequins, too, can be added while building up the picture to give more depth and to almost disguise them so that they fit perfectly with the composition of the piece.

VARNISHING

Many of the projects in this book haven't been varnished, as the subjects that are decoupaged are quite delicate. However, with furniture and solid objects it's advisable to varnish them, for protection and sheen. The best type of varnish to use on paper is acrylic varnish, available to paint or spray. With both types of varnish it is advisable to apply the varnish a small amount at a time, using several thin coats rather than one or two thick coats. Keep the varnished surface free of dust and dirt in between layers.

SALT DOUGH

Salt dough shapes make attractive decorations for gifts, and will last indefinitely. They can be painted, varnished or simply left plain.

YOU WILL NEED

- *2 cups (450ml) plain white flour*
- *1 cup (225ml) salt*
- *2 tablespoons (30ml) wallpaper paste*
- *poster paints or varnish*

1 Combine the salt, flour and wallpaper paste. Add water gradually, mixing first with a fork and then using your hand, until the dough is stiff but not sticky.

2 Turn the dough out onto a work surface and knead for about ten minutes, until smooth.

3 To prevent the dough from drying out, keep it wrapped in plastic wrap until you are ready to use it.

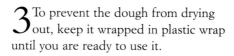
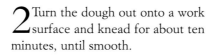
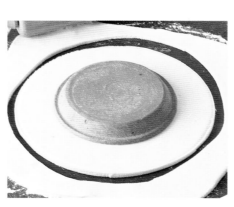

4 On a lightly floured surface, roll out the dough to a thickness of ¼in (6mm).

5 Use to cut out shapes, either using a template as a guide or cut out freehand. Using a skewer, make a hole at the top of each shape. Bake at 225°F (110°C/Gas Mark 1/4) for eight hours until the shapes are completely dry. Leave to cool then decorate as desired.

PAPER TOLE PANSY

This realistic-looking flower is very easy to make, and is perfect

for embellishing any surface.

YOU WILL NEED

- *Pencil*
- *Template*
- *Tracing paper*
- *Background paper*
- *Small scissors*
- *Molding tool*
- *Glue*
- *Foam tape*
- *Small tweezers*

1 Using a soft pencil, trace the template onto a sheet of tracing paper. Turn the tracing paper over and outline the design again. Place the tracing paper onto the chosen background and secure with tape. Trace the design once more.

2 Lift off the tracing paper – the design will be transferred to the background paper.

3 Carefully cut out three sets of the colored pansy piece, trimming each piece as closely as possible, so that there is no white paper visible around the edges. N.B. When cutting out pieces, don't snip; turn the print and feed it into the scissors.

4 Using a molding tool, shape two sets of the leaves and petals on the wrong side. (Keep one set flat for the base.) Use small circular movements around the edge and shape so that they lose their flatness.

5 Glue the first layer of leaves and buds onto the base design.

7 Build up the flowers, adding height with either large drops of glue or small pieces of foam tape inserted between the layers.

8 Use small tweezers to handle petals and to place pieces accurately into position.

6 Glue down the second layer of leaves and buds. To create depth and dimension to the leaves, add large drops of glue, and add more if necessary, then position the next leaf. Position and glue the third layer of leaves and buds.

STATIONERY
AND
GIFT WRAP

Gift tags, envelopes, boxes and
greetings cards are just some of the
delightful items that can be embellished
with three-dimensional decoupage, using
lace, beads, sequins, floral scraps, doilies
and shaped motifs.

LACY HAND-CRAFTED ENVELOPES

For Victorian couples, courting was often done by way of secret notes and love letters sent in elaborately decorated envelopes. These envelopes are reminiscent of the kind of stationery used. They have been cut from hand-made paper, then edged in delicate tea-stained lace.

YOU WILL NEED

- *Natural hand-made paper*
- *Pencil and eraser*
- *Scissors*
- *Glue*
- *Thin lace edging*
- *Paper doily*
- *Gold spray paint*
- *Gold paper leaves*
- *Sealing wax*

1 Copy the template from page 104 onto the back of the paper, making sure that the folding lines are perfectly straight. The solid lines will be cut and the dotted lines are folded.

2 Cut out the main shape, including the scalloped edges of the envelope flap, and fold along the fold lines, so that they are sharp and neat. Unfold the envelope and erase the pencil lines around the edges and on the folds.

Refold the envelope with the bottom flap underneath and the two short diagonal sides on top. Glue them down, using a minimum amount of glue.

3 Stain the lace by dipping it into a cup of tea or coffee and allowing it to dry. Cut a piece of the lace edging to fit along both sides of the envelope flap. Glue it to the flap along the inside of the envelope. The scalloped side should be sticking out from under the flap.

4 Spray the doily with the gold paint and allow to dry. Cut small elements from the doily, arrange them around the envelope, and glue down. One of these small cut-outs could also go on the back flap of the envelope.

5 Build up the doilies by cutting out smaller elements and sticking them down on top of the previous ones. Finally, glue a gold leaf down on the envelope flap to use as a closing. When you are ready to use the envelope, use sealing wax to hold the flap closed.

HEARTS AND STARS GIFT TAGS

These unusual little gift tags are made from salt dough shapes decoupaged with floral scraps and beads. They are attached to a larger cardboard shape with a length of pretty ribbon. These could be made using any simple shapes.

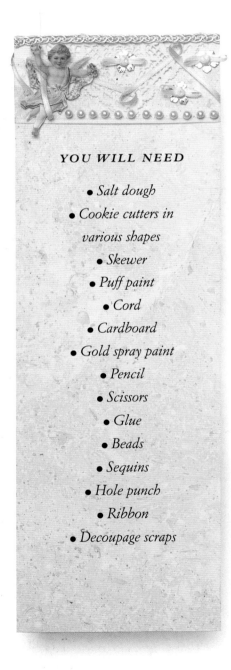

YOU WILL NEED

- Salt dough
- Cookie cutters in various shapes
- Skewer
- Puff paint
- Cord
- Cardboard
- Gold spray paint
- Pencil
- Scissors
- Glue
- Beads
- Sequins
- Hole punch
- Ribbon
- Decoupage scraps

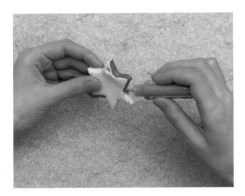

1 Prepare the salt dough (recipe on page 19) and cut out with the cookie cutters; stars and hearts were used here. Push a skewer through the top of each shape to make a hole, then bake to set and harden. When cool, outline the edges of the shapes with the puff paint, or glue a decorative cord around the edges.

3 Cut out tiny decoupage motifs for each shape and glue them onto the salt dough shapes, allowing a little of the image to extend over the edge. Add beads and sequins to the salt dough and cardboard shapes to give a little sparkle.

2 Using the template from page 105 as a guide, draw slightly larger shapes onto the cardboard. Cut them out and spray both sides with gold paint.

4 Punch a hole in a corner of the shapes. Thread a ribbon through the salt dough shape and its cardboard shape, with the decoupaged salt dough shape at the front. Write your message onto the back of the card.

ANGEL PORTFOLIO FOLDER

Angels are always a popular motif with adults and children alike.

This project would make a very useful gift.

YOU WILL NEED

- Thin cardboard
- Thick Bristol paper or hand-made paper
- Marbled paper
- Cream-colored doilies
- Angel printed floral ribbon
- Gold elastic cord
- Glue
- Transparent tape
- Dimensional paint
- Scissors/craft knife
- Cutting mat

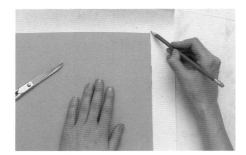

1 Cut two identical pieces of cardboard 8½ × 11 inches (A4 sized). Place the two pieces side by side onto a sheet of thick paper and cut around the outside of the two pieces of cardboard, leaving an allowance for folding over the edges. Do not cut down the middle of the paper, between the two pieces. Fold the paper in half to form the portfolio shape.

2 Remove the two pieces of cardboard from the paper and cover one side of each piece with the soft marbled paper. You can tape it down on the back side, as only one side will be showing.

3 Place the covered boards back into the cover, with taped sides facing down. Apply fabric glue to lengths of floral ribbon and bind the edges of the cardboard and the paper together on the right side, then on the left, so that the card is stuck inside the folder.

4 Turn the portfolio so that the front side is facing up, and decorate with the doilies and dimensional paint.

5 Finally, glue gold elastic cord onto the top and bottom right-hand corners, to create a way to open and close the portfolio folder.

INITIALLED GIFT BOX

This tiny gift box is as special as the gift it holds. The lid of the box features a three-dimensional Gothic initial, surrounded by pearl beads and silky cord.

YOU WILL NEED

- Initial, photocopied from a book
- Silver acrylic paint
- Thin cardboard
- Small round box
- White paint
- Small piece of white organza or other sheer material
- Strong glue
- Scissors
- Paper doily
- Large oval pearl beads
- White cord
- Foam tape
- Small pearl beads

1 Photocopy two initials and then paint them with a watered-down, almost transparent layer of silver acrylic paint; allow to dry.

2 Once the paint has completely dried, glue both initials onto a piece of thin cardboard. Cut one initial as a square and the other as the shape of the letter. Put the initials aside while you work on the rest of the box.

3 Paint the box and lid with the white paint. Begin by covering the lid with the white organza. To do this, lay the lid upside down on the fabric and cut it so that it is slightly larger than the lid. Put a dot of glue on the center of the lid top and secure the fabric onto it. Cut tabs

around the excess fabric and glue them down around the edge of the lid. Then take a strip of the fabric and cover the tabs around the edge by winding it around and gluing into place.

4 Cut out circular shapes from a paper doily and glue them around the base of the box, interspersing each shape with a large pearl bead.

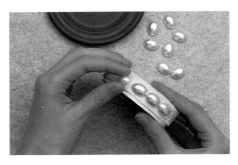

5 Glue the large pearl beads around the edge of the lid, keeping them close together. Then cover the fabric joins with a length of white cord, one along the top rim and one along the lower rim.

6 Put foam tape pads onto the back of the squared-off initial, and glue it onto the center of the box lid so that it stands up in relief against the flat, round lid. Select small pearl beads and glue them onto the lid, framing the initial. To save time, string the beads before gluing them on the lid.

7 Finally, take the cut-out initial, stick a piece of foam tape onto its back and attach it to the first initial, putting it exactly over the letter so that it looks as if the initial is three-dimensional.

ROSEBUD GIFT-WRAPPED BOX

This is a simple idea which can be done to a box of any shape or size. The motifs are hearts and stars which have been cut from a good quality paper. The layered shapes have a stair-like quality about them. You could use initials instead of motifs for the top of the box to personalize it.

YOU WILL NEED

- *A small square box*
- *Wrapping paper to wrap box, if necessary*
- *Scissors*
- *Lace*
- *Glue*
- *Thick Bristol paper*
- *Silver acrylic paint*
- *Paintbrush*
- *Craft knife*
- *Foam tape*
- *Ribbon*
- *Dried rose heads*

1 Cover the box if it needs to be covered. Use a soft, muted gift wrapping paper and miter the corners to give a neat and smooth finish. Cut a length of lace and glue it along the inside rim of the box lid, making sure that the scalloped edge sticks out from the lid.

2 Neatly tear two squares of Bristol paper, so that each covers one quarter of the box lid.

3 Using the templates provided, draw three heart and three star shapes, one in each size, onto a piece of thick Bristol paper. Paint them silver and cut out.

4 Place foam tape on the reverse of the motifs. Place the small heart on the middle heart, and then stick the middle heart on the large heart. Center them onto one of the squares of paper. Repeat this with the star shapes and the other square of paper.

5 Glue the paper squares with the heart and star raised motifs onto the box, placing them at opposing corners. Tie a thin, blue ribbon around the box, dividing it into quarters. Finally, place the tiny dried rose heads into the ribbon bow at the center of the box lid.

FLORAL GREETING CARDS

Cards cut with windows can make wonderful greeting cards. Instead of framing the window with motifs, as on the menu cards on page 38, use the frame as the frame of the picture. Glue an assortment of flowers inside the oval or round window, so that they actually go over the window edge when the card is eventually folded up.

YOU WILL NEED

- *Paper doily*
- *Gold spray paint*
- *Card blank, with a round window*
- *Glue*
- *Scissors*
- *Floral decoupage scraps*
- *Gold outliner paint*

1 Spray the doily with the gold paint and allow to dry. Cut it to fit around the round window with the scalloped edges facing out. Then carefully cut out the center and the sides so that it fits over the card. Glue into place.

3 Mark off the round shape on the inside of the card with a pencil. Glue down decoupage scraps within the circular shape. When the circle is covered, attach flowers at the inside point, and turn and curl them up so they stand out from the window.

2 Select flowers from your decoupage scraps, choosing those that are more or less of the same size and similar colors. Begin to arrange them in the center of the card – the part which isn't covered in doily.

4 Finally, frame the round window and the whole card with tiny swirls of gold outliner paint to give the card an extra dimension.

BAROQUE PRESENTATION BOX

Even an old wooden cheese box can be made to look special with three-dimensional decoupage. Here, a classic image is framed with delicate bits of gold doily.

YOU WILL NEED

- Round box
- Gold acrylic paint
- Paintbrush
- Gold spray paint
- Paper doilies
- Decoupage scrap or picture of classic painting
- PVA glue
- Silicone glue
- Decorative braids and tassels in gold and bronze
- Scissors

1 If the box isn't gold, begin by painting a couple of even coats of the gold acrylic onto its entire surface. Spray paint a couple of doilies while you want for the paint to dry.

3 Taking the curved elements from the gold doily, cut them out and arrange them around the motif, with the curved sides facing in, so that the opening forms a star shape. Glue down.

2 Select a classic image to fit into the lid of the box. Cut it out and glue it down firmly, pressing out all the air bubbles as you do so.

4 Glue tiny doily shapes around the frame. Using silicone glue will make them stand up in relief. Add gold braid to finish.

BUTTERFLY MENU CARDS

Window cards make ideal menu cards, since the dishes of the day can be removed and replaced without damaging the embellishments. Frame the card with butterflies, then edge it with fine lace ribbon and delicate pearls to finish it off in a professional way.

YOU WILL NEED

- *Paper doily*
- *Card with rectangular cut-out*
- *Thin lace*
- *Butterfly scraps (two of each image)*
- *Sharp scissors*
- *Glue*
- *Large pearl beads*
- *Tiny pearl beads*

1 Place the doily over the front of the card and then cut the doily so that it is exactly the same size as the card. Cut out the window, so that the doily looks like a lacy frame.

2 Edge the outside edge of the card and the inside frame of the window with the thin lace. This will neaten and even out the edges of the card.

3 Cut out the decoupage scraps of the butterflies, making sure that you cut out at least two each of the same motif. Gently fold back the wings on the first set of motifs, and apply glue along the center, where the butterfly body is. Glue the first motifs down along the edge of the card.

4 Bend over the wings on the second set of butterflies, put glue along the center, where the butterfly body is, and stick over the first set of butterflies. Curl the wings back, so that it looks as though they are about to take off. Add finishing touches by sticking down little pieces of doily and the pearl beads in various places around the card.

SPECIAL OCCASIONS

A gift that has been made especially for the recipient is always welcome. Three-dimensional decoupage transforms everyday baskets, wreaths, tins, hats and even Easter eggs to make decorative and personalized presents.

FABERGE STYLE EASTER EGGS

These fabulous eggs show what you can do with polystyrene egg shapes, available at most craft shops. It is so easy to make luxurious and fantastic Easter eggs by simply wrapping them in papers, ribbons and sequins.

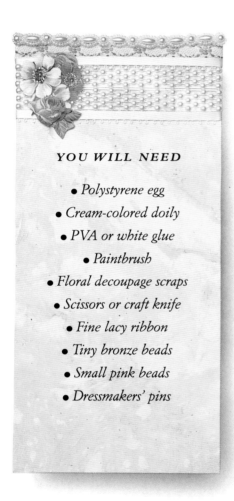

YOU WILL NEED

- Polystyrene egg
- Cream-colored doily
- PVA or white glue
- Paintbrush
- Floral decoupage scraps
- Scissors or craft knife
- Fine lacy ribbon
- Tiny bronze beads
- Small pink beads
- Dressmakers' pins

1 Cut strips from the doily, so that you have several long, thin pieces with scalloped edges.

2 Glue the strips onto the egg lengthwise. Lay the first strip on so that it lies flat against the surface. Glue down the remaining strips with the scalloped edges unglued, so that they stand up in relief to the background.

3 Cut out the decoupage scraps and glue them into position onto the center of the egg. Build up from here, if you wish to. Glue the motifs down in the middle and curl up the edges so that they stand out from the egg.

4 Take a length of ribbon and pin it to the bottom of the egg. Wind the ribbon around the egg, sectioning it off into six equal parts, using the pin at the bottom and one at the top of the egg to keep the ribbon secure.

5 Add extra embellishments by threading dressmakers' pins each with a tiny bronze and a small pink bead. Push these into the polystyrene egg, in rows or at occasional points.

VARIATION

By varying the ribbons, decoupage scraps, spray paint and decorative touches you can create a whole range of beautiful eggs.

YOU WILL NEED

- *Polystyrene egg*
- *Paper doily*
- *Silver spray paint*
- *Scissors*
- *Glue*
- *Straight pins*
- *Thin white ribbon*
- *Pearl beads*
- *Silver dimensional paint*
- *Sheer and metallic ribbon*

1 Spray the doily with the silver paint. When using spray paint, work in a well-ventilated area, with the work surfaces covered in scrap paper. Once the paint has dried, cut the doily into smaller pieces.

2 Apply glue to the polystyrene egg and press the small doily pieces onto the surface of the egg, snipping and trimming the paper if needed, to create a smooth surface.

3 Pin a thin white ribbon to the top of the egg and then proceed to wind the ribbon around the egg as shown, sectioning it off into eight parts.

4 Thread the pearl beads onto the pins and insert them in four equally spaced rows between the lines of ribbon. Push them all the way in so that only the beads are visible.

5 Using three-dimensional puff paint, paint tiny dots along the white ribbon, so that they stand up in relief to the background.

6 Finally, make a full bow out of a sheer and metallic ribbon to pin onto the top of the egg.

VENETIAN NEW YEAR'S EVE MASK

Inspired by the masked balls of Venice, this mask is simply a piece of cardboard which has been embellished with paint, doilies, beads, and fantastic orange feathers. Ideal for a fancy dress party or as a decorative ornament for the wall.

YOU WILL NEED

- *Cardboard*
- *Pencil*
- *Tracing paper*
- *Craft knife*
- *Dark blue acrylic paint*
- *Paintbrush*
- *Paper doily*
- *Gold spray paint*
- *Gold outliner paint*
- *Glue*
- *Multicolored plastic jewels*
- *Orange feathers, from a feather duster*

1 Using the template on page 107, trace the eye mask onto a piece of cardboard cut from a heavy-duty box.

2 Carefully cut out the mask using a craft knife. Cut in long smooth strokes, being particularly careful when you are cutting out the eyes.

3 Paint both sides of the mask with a dark blue paint. Two coats will suffice, but allow the first coat to dry completely before painting the next.

4 Spray the doily with gold paint and allow to dry. Cut single curved elements from the doily that fit exactly

beneath the cut-out eyes, and glue them into place. Place another piece of doily underneath the mask, positioning it so that the curved edges poke out along the bottom. Trim the doily, and glue along the lower edge of the mask.

5 Outline the cut-out eyes with a smooth line of gold outliner paint. This will make the eye holes more noticeable and dramatic.

6 Arrange the plastic jewels along the top area of the mask and glue into place. Using the gold outliner paint, dot specks of gold in between the jewels.

7 Pick orange feathers off a feather duster, dip the ends of the feathers into a pot of glue and push the ends into the holes at the edge of the cardboard. Fill the entire top edge of the mask with feathers. To finish off, line the upper edge of the mask, between the feathers and the mask, with the gold outliner.

CHINESE NEW YEAR TIN

An old chocolate or cookie tin with the labels washed off has been covered in gold doilies, glass beads and sequins. This selection of embellishments gives a plain tin an exotic touch.

YOU WILL NEED

- *Paper doily*
- *Gold spray paint*
- *Scissors*
- *Red rectangular-shaped tin*
- *Glue*
- *Gold outliner paint*
- *Paintbrush*
- *Glass beads*
- *Gold flower sequins*
- *Gold beaded cord (optional)*

1 Spray the doily with gold paint. When dry, cut out various attractive elements. Arrange them around the tin, covering the corners and flat spaces; glue them into position.

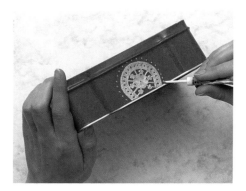

2 Once the doilies have dried into place, use the gold outliner paint and paint dots around the doily shapes.

3 Select some glass beads and small flower sequins; add these onto the gold doily patterns at random.

4 If using, choose a piece of gold beaded cord that is thin enough to be stuck around the edge of the lid comfortably. Glue it into position, ensuring that it goes all around the box and that the ends are tied off neatly.

5 Finally, if you feel that the tin needs even more embellishment, glue tiny glass beads around the tin at occasional points and/or in patterns.

CHRISTMAS CUPID WREATH

A cane wreath, available from most florists, is usually covered in plants and flowers. Here we've given it a decoupage treatment, and covered it in both sheer and lace ribbon. Angels and cupids are attached in layers to give a three-dimensional look.

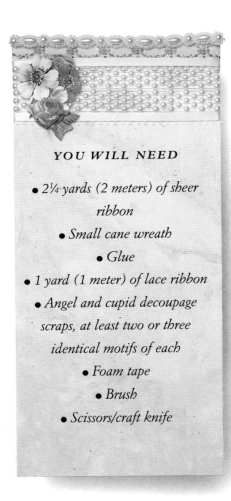

YOU WILL NEED

- 2¼ yards (2 meters) of sheer ribbon
- Small cane wreath
- Glue
- 1 yard (1 meter) of lace ribbon
- Angel and cupid decoupage scraps, at least two or three identical motifs of each
- Foam tape
- Brush
- Scissors/craft knife

1 Pull one end of the sheer ribbon through into a cane branch and tie it to secure, then wind the whole length of it around the wreath, covering the cane completely.

2 Put a tiny amount of glue on one end of the lace ribbon, secure at a point on the wreath and proceed to wind it around the wreath on top of the sheer ribbon, allowing the sheer ribbon to be seen in between the lace.

3 Cut out five angels and cupids of various sizes, with at least three of each variety.

4 If you have one motif with three identical images, first cut out an entire angel, then add arms, legs, body and flowers, layering these on top of one another and sticking them down with foam tape, to achieve a three-dimensional effect.

5 Arrange all five angels and cupids around the wreath and once you are happy with the composition, glue them into place.

6 Finally, make a bow from the sheer or lace ribbon and attach it to the top of the wreath, tie it into place and leave an extra length to hang it from.

THANKSGIVING WREATH

For this attractive wreath, leaves are painted in autumn hues, then together with berries and nuts, are used as a rich embellishment.

YOU WILL NEED

- *Cane wreath*
- *Acrylic paints in brown, green, orange and gold*
- *Paintbrushes*
- *Florists' wire*
- *Artificial leaves and berries*
- *Black and white photocopies of leaves*
- *Thin cardboard*
- *White glue*
- *Scissors/craft knife*
- *Glue gun*
- *Nuts*
- *Gold gilt wax*

1 Paint the cane wreath with two coats of dark brown acrylic paint. Allow the first coat to dry before going on to do the next. Use the brush in stabbing motions to get the paint into all the nooks and crannies.

2 Using the florists' wire, carefully wind the artificial branch of the leaves and berries around the cane wreath. Hold it in position by looping florists' wire through the branch and then through the wreath, then twisting the ends together to hold firmly in place.

3 Paint the black and white photocopies of leaves with a wash of the various autumnal acrylic paints. Allow these to dry and then carefully glue them onto a thin sheet of cardboard.

4 Carefully cut out these new autumn leaves, using a sharp pair of scissors or a craft knife.

5 Heat up the glue gun and attach the cardboard leaves to the wreath, fitting the cardboard leaves in among the artificial leaves and berries.

6 Apply gold gilt wax to a selection of nuts. We used hazel nuts, brazil nuts and walnuts. Simply dip a soft cloth into a jar of wax and wipe the wax onto the nuts; it will dry within a matter of minutes. Finally, using the hot glue gun, attach the nuts to the wreath, arranging them in among the artificial leaves and berries and the cardboard leaves.

RETIREMENT "FOREST OF FLOWERS" PICTURE GIFT

Boxes with window lids are ideal for displaying three-dimensional decoupage pictures. This particular picture is made up of a variety of pink flowers that have been layered and turned and curled to create a wonderfully overgrown display.

YOU WILL NEED

- *Box with window lid*
- *Light green paint*
- *Paper doily*
- *Decoupage scraps of pink flowers*
- *Magazine and catalog pictures of pink flowers*
- *Foam tape*
- *PVA glue*
- *Paintbrush*
- *Scissors and/or craft knife*
- *Tiny shell sequins*

1 Paint the outside of the box with a light green paint. Cut the center out of a doily, using its scalloped edging as a guide, then trim it to fit into the window. Glue it face down onto the window lid to create a lacy edging.

2 Cut out various pink flowers and, starting with the larger images, build up a picture by just arranging them to achieve the desired composition.

3 Glue down the larger pictures onto the base of the box. Press the motifs down, smoothing away any air bubbles or excess glue.

4 Begin to build up the layers, gluing only parts of the motif and curling the sections that aren't glued down. Add the motifs that you want to be in the foreground. Use pieces of foam tape, one on top of the other, attached to the back of the motifs, so that they will stand up in relief.

5 Decorate the edge of the glass lid by gluing down tiny shell sequins, which look iridescent when they catch the light. Place the lid on top of the picture to complete the project.

MOTHERS' DAY PANSY BASKET

An otherwise plain, yet elegant, fluted glass basket has been made a little more special with the addition of pansies and roses around the base. The handle has been covered in gold paper leaves with wire stems, and tied securely with an elaborate chiffon bow.

YOU WILL NEED

- *Flower decoupage scraps*
  - *PVA glue*
- *Fluted glass basket*
  - *Paintbrush*
  - *Craft knife*
  - *Foam tape*
- *Gold paper leaves with wire stems*
- *Sheer ribbon with gold edging*

1 Carefully cut out the flower scraps. The flowers should be small enough to fit along the sides of the basket, not so big that they overpower the shape. Arrange the flowers to see how the composition will look.

3 Add foam tape to those scraps that you want to be three-dimensional and attach them to the basket on and around the flowers. Curl up the petals to make them stand out from the background.

2 Apply PVA glue to the back of the scraps. Glue these to the front of the basket, facing out. Do not worry about the PVA glue being opaque as it will dry transparent.

4 Take the gold leaves and wrap the wire stems around the handle of the basket, moving the leaves to cover the handle and the visible wires.

5 Tie a ribbon around the handle, covering as much of the wire as you can, and tie a huge bow in the center.

EASTER BONNET

This simple straw hat has been transformed into a charming decorative wallhanging. Clusters of three-dimensional flowers have been attached around the crown and the brim, then finished off with ribbons and voile rosettes.

YOU WILL NEED

- Straw bonnet
- Lacy ribbon
- Needle and thread
- Flowery ribbon
- Sheer roses
- Floral decoupage scraps
- Foam tape
- Fabric glue
- Tiny satin roses
- Thin pink satin ribbon

1 Take a length of lacy ribbon and sew it around the brim of a straw bonnet, catching one side of the lace to the hat with tiny stitches.

2 Measure around the base of the crown and cut a length of the flowery ribbon to that size. Sew on the sheer roses at intervals along the ribbon, and then stitch it into place around the lower part of the crown.

3 Cut out the decoupage flower motifs. Attach them to each other in small clusters using foam tape, so that they are held together but stand slightly away from each other.

4 Begin to glue these three-dimensional flowers to the front of the hat, so there is a cluster on the crown and the brim.

5 Sew the occasional tiny satin rose in and around the cluster of paper flowers to give an even more three-dimensional effect. To finish off, wind the thin pink ribbon around the base of the crown, at the bottom edge of the first ribbon, to hold some of the decoupage flowers in place at the bottom.

FURNITURE

The simplest household objects such as mirrors,
fireguards, picture frames, clocks and letter racks
can be given unique flourishes by applying three-
dimensional decoupage. Motifs, pearl beads, lace
and buttons are used to stunning effect.

PEARLY KINGS PICTURE FRAME

Any plain purchased picture frame can be easily transformed. This one is decorated by simply covering the frame with glue and adding a variety of white and cream buttons interspersed with tiny pearl beads.

YOU WILL NEED

- *Picture frame*
- *Variety of cream and white buttons*
- *Pearl beads*
- *Glue*
- *Scissors*
- *Square, cream-colored paper doily*
- *Gold outliner paint*

1 Cover the entire frame with a generous layer of glue and place a whole variety of different buttons all over the surface.

3 Trim the edges off a square doily to get pieces that are about an inch wide and long enough to fit along the outside edges of the frame. Fold them in half lengthwise, apply glue along the outside edges of the frame, and press the pieces into position.

2 Once the bulk of the surface is covered you may find there are lots of smaller spaces which are too small for buttons. Place pearl beads into these smaller spaces.

4 To finish off the picture frame, pipe the edges of the inner and outer frame with the gold outliner paint.

GOLD LEAVES PICTURE FRAME

This frame is extremely simple to make. Real leaves have been glued in a decorative pattern onto the frame, which is then covered in gold gilt wax.

YOU WILL NEED

- *Small leaves collected from a garden*
- *Clean paper*
- *Glue*
- *Paintbrush*
- *Picture frame*
- *Soft cloth or kitchen towel*
- *Gold gilt wax*
- *Tiny glass rocaille beads*
- *Spray acrylic varnish*

1 Select your leaves from the garden, snip off the stem and allow to dry for a couple of hours on a piece of clean paper. Paint the front of the leaves with glue and attach face down onto the frame. Sticking them face down allows the veins on the back of the leaves to stand out.

2 Using a soft cloth or a kitchen towel, begin to wax the frame, dipping the cloth in the jar of wax and wiping it onto the frame. Don't overload the frame, as it is better to build up the wax in layers.

3 Allow the wax to dry, and then add a second coat of wax to the frame. When adding wax to the leaves, carefully pat the gold wax onto the leaves, being careful not to tear them.

4 Allow this next coat to dry and then apply the final coat of wax, rubbing it into the surface of the frame to give it a burnished look.

5 Apply a little dot of glue at the stem point of each leaf, and stick on the tiny glass rocaille beads.

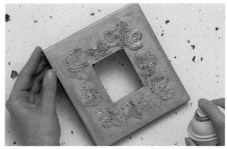

6 Finally, using a spray acrylic varnish, spray one layer of the varnish over the gold leaves and frame.

DECORATIVE SHELF UNIT

A blank knickknacks shelf has been painted with two different colors, and then sanded lightly, to achieve a distressed look. Fruits of the forest have been decoupaged around the top and lower edges of the unit, with their greenery flowing down.

YOU WILL NEED

- *A blank pressed wood shelf unit*
- *Dark green and lighter green latex paint*
- *White latex paint*
- *Sandpaper*
- *Old rag*
- *Paintbrush*
- *Pictures of grapes & apples color photocopied from magazines*
- *Scissors/craft knife*
- *Cutting mat*
- *Glue*
- *Decoupage varnish*
- *Gold outliner paint*
- *Foam tape*

1 Paint the unit with two coats of dark green latex paint, allow to dry and then apply a coat of lighter green paint. Allow this to dry thoroughly before starting the next step.

2 Lightly sand the top layer of green paint to reveal the darker color beneath it. If the colors look too vivid and you wish to tone them down slightly, simply water down some white latex, paint it over the surface and quickly wipe it off with an old rag.

3 Cut out your images of fruit, using a pair of scissors. You may wish to use a really sharp craft knife for the more intricate parts. Arrange the images across the front of the unit with the larger fruits at the bottom, the smaller ones at the top and the leaves falling down the sides.

4 Glue the larger images down flat on the unit, smoothing out the air bubbles with your thumb to keep them flat. If the bubbles prove difficult to remove, simply prick the bubble with a pin and ease the air out. Varnish the flat images using decoupage varnish, which will paint on opaque and white, but will dry transparent.

5 Start layering the fruits over the base, using foam tape to give them height against the flat surface of the unit. Allow the tendrils to fall free over the lower edge of the unit.

MANDOLIN AND VIOLETS CLOCK

A plain, unpainted carriage clock bought from a chain store has been changed into a pretty, music-inspired time piece. We painted it in a soft lilac color and then built up the mandolin and violets into three-dimensional images.

YOU WILL NEED

- *Plain wood-encased clock*
- *Lilac latex or acrylic paint*
- *Paintbrush*
- *Three identical images of mandolin*
- *Violets decoupage scraps*
- *Scissors/craft knife*
- *Cutting mat*
- *Silicone glue*
- *Pearl puff paint*

1 Paint the clock surround with the lilac-colored paint. Use two to three coats to make a smooth and even finish.

2 Cut out the mandolins and the flowers. Cut out the first mandolin in its entirety, including the flowery background. From the second one, cut out just the instrument, and from the third cut out just the strings. Also cut out tiny flowers for the clock.

3 Using silicone glue, build up the mandolin before it goes on the clock, attaching the strings to the mandolin and then the mandolin to the one with the floral background. Also, build up flowers to go behind the mandolin, to create a floral background.

4 Glue the mandolin and flowers onto the lower part of the clock.

5 Using the silicone glue, attach the tiny flowers around the clock face at every three hours. Pipe dots of pearl puff paint around the clock face.

MESSENGER'S LETTER RACK

A blank letter rack with heart cut-outs has been painted in a soft blue and then embellished with three-dimensional paper forget-me-nots and roses. The final touch are the swallows, who are traditionally used as messengers.

YOU WILL NEED

- *A pressed wood blank letter rack*
- *Light blue latex paint*
- *Paintbrush*
- *Pink puff paint*
- *Floral and bird decoupage scraps*
- *Scissors/craft knife*
- *Cutting mat*
- *Foam tape*
- *Glue*
- *Blue satin ribbon roses*

1 Paint the letter rack with the light blue paint; do two or three coats to give a smooth and even finish. If after the second coat, it looks lumpy, sand it down lightly before doing the third coat.

2 Pierce the top of the puff paint tube with a pin, and carefully pipe the paint around the insides of all four of the hearts. Pipe dots around the center of the two hearts, that won't have decoupage around them.

3 Cut out the flowers to fit around the top and lower heart cutouts. Arrange them around the hearts as you cut, building up a composition.

4 When you are satisfied with the composition, glue the base of the decoupage down. Then, using pieces of foam tape, begin to layer the flower motifs on top of the base.

5 Cut out the birds, cutting a second, identical set of wings for each. Attach the second set of wings to each cut-out with foam tape, so that they look three-dimensional. Once you have achieved the right look, glue them into the correct place.

6 Finally, add a couple of blue satin ribbon roses to the decoupaged flowers on the top and lower hearts. Secure them with glue.

BUTTERFLY SHELF EDGING

Shelf edging is often crocheted, but here we have used a beautiful soft marbled paper as its base and created a crocheted effect by adding paper lace from a doily. The butterflies appear to be in motion, with glittery antennae and bodies.

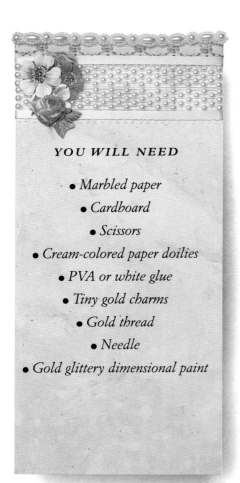

YOU WILL NEED

- *Marbled paper*
- *Cardboard*
- *Scissors*
- *Cream-colored paper doilies*
- *PVA or white glue*
- *Tiny gold charms*
- *Gold thread*
- *Needle*
- *Gold glittery dimensional paint*

1 Fold the paper along its length to a suitable size to fit on your shelf. Make a cardboard pattern from the template on page 108, then draw around it along the folded edge of the paper, repeating it as you go along.

2 Using a sharp pair of scissors, carefully cut out along the drawn lines, creating a pointed scallop along the flap of the shelf edging.

3 Cut out sections of the doily and fit them in between the peaks of the scallops so that the decorative edge shows; glue them into place.

4 Once the doily shapes have dried into position, sew the tiny charms onto the lower edge of the doily. Use fine gold thread and a needle to sew them, making sure that each charm is at the center lower edge of the doily piece.

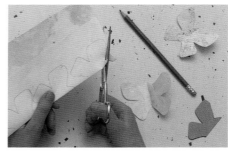

5 Using the butterfly template on page 108, cut out as many butterflies as you need to fit along the scalloped edges. Cut two for each part, as one will be placed on top of the other.

6 Fold one butterfly from each pair in half, then open it out and glue it on top of its partner, placing the glue along the folded line. Glue the butterflies into place along the edge. Using glittery paint, add antennae and bodies.

PRESERVE JAR LABELS

When making your home-made preserves and jams, make your own three-dimensional labels by adding images of the fruits that are in the preserves. Just attach them from the sides and let the leaves and branches curl off the edge.

YOU WILL NEED

- *Empty jars*
- *Plain paper or card*
- *Fruit and flowers decoupage scraps*
- *Glue*
- *Foam tape*
- *Scissors/craft knife*
- *Cutting mat*
- *Gingham scrap*
- *Ribbon, cord or other trim*

1 Cut the paper or card to the size you wish the label to be. Select your fruit images and cut them out carefully, keeping them small so that they frame the label rather than dominate it.

2 Start the decoupage by gluing the base fruit scraps down around the label. Proceed to build up the decoupage around the label, using the foam tape to give the top layers height and to differentiate between the background and the foreground.

3 Using a pair of sharp scissors, cut a circle out of the gingham fabric that is large enough to cover the top of the jar, but small enough so that the overhang isn't too long. If desired, embellish the edge with cord.

4 Finally, attach the label and place the gingham circle over the jar top and tie into place with a co-ordinating cord.

PLAYING CATS FIREPLACE SCREEN

This fireplace screen is the ideal housewarming gift for cat-loving friends. Black and white photocopies have been washed with watered-down acrylics, although watercolors will do just as well. These frolicking cats were painted to look like tabbies.

YOU WILL NEED

- *Pressed wood fireplace screen*
- *Light and dark burgundy latex paint*
- *Gold, orange and brown acrylic paints*
- *Black and white photocopies of playing cats, at least three of each*
- *Scissors*
- *Thin cardboard*
- *PVA or white glue*
- *Fabric glue*
- *Fabric scrap*
- *Batting scrap*
- *Silicone rubber glue*
- *Orange yarn*
- *A selection of paintbrushes*

1 First paint the fireplace screen. Using watered-down acrylic colors, paint the photocopies with a mixture of browns and oranges to make the cats resemble tabbies. If the picture finishes awkwardly, as you can see one cat has had its back cut, simply draw in the missing parts with a pencil and paint over it. Cut out roughly.

2 Keep two complete cats aside for the base layer. Cut details from other copies and glue them firmly onto thin cardboard. Arrange the cats into position in the center of the screen, but don't glue them. Once in place, position the fabric in the corner, so that one of the cats is sitting on it. Cut it to the required size. Mark where the ball of yarn will go.

3 Cut the batting a couple of inches smaller than the fabric, then glue it down firmly on the board. Place the fabric over the batting and secure that into place with the fabric glue.

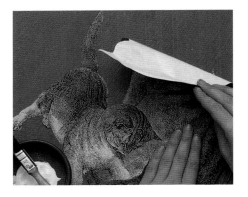

4 Glue the base layer of cats down onto the board. The part where the cat is sitting on the cushion will not adhere, but make sure the rest of the cats are stuck down firmly.

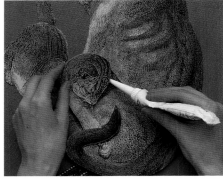

5 Build up the cats on the base layer, placing the cardboard details into position then securing them with the silicone rubber glue, so that they stand up in relief.

6 Paint the area that you have marked
for the ball of yarn with fabric glue,
then wind the yarn into a ball shape
onto the board.

DRESSING ROOM MIRROR

A pretty yet plain tortoiseshell-handled mirror has been given a three-dimensional decoupage treatment by the simple addition of flowers, ribbons and a touch of paint.

YOU WILL NEED

- Scissors/craft knife
- Floral decoupage scraps
- Cutting mat
- Silicone rubber glue
- Handled mirror
- Glue
- Paintbrush
- Acrylic varnish
- Thin ribbon
- Dimensional paint

1 Using scissors or a craft knife, cut out a variety of floral scraps on a cutting mat and proceed to build them up onto each other, using tiny blobs of silicone rubber glue to stick them together while giving them height.

2 Arrange the built-up clusters of flowers onto the back of the mirror. When you have created a pleasing composition, secure them into place with glue.

3 Once the glue has dried, carefully varnish all the paper scraps with acrylic varnish. This will give them a sheen as well as harden the surface.

4 Tie tiny bows of the thin ribbon, cutting the ends so that they trail slightly, then glue these into place in and among the floral scraps.

5 Finally, using the dimensional paint, pipe dots around the decoupaged composition to frame the work.

DECORATIVE BIRDHOUSE

On this decorative birdhouse, the front is embellished with hovering doves and the edges with snowdrops and violets.

YOU WILL NEED

- Small decorative birdhouse
- Blue acrylic paint
- Paintbrush
- Decoupage scraps of doves (at least two of each)
- Snowdrops and floral decoupage borders
- Scissors/craft knife
- Cutting mat
- Silicone glue
- Pencil

1 Paint the birdhouse with blue paint and set aside to dry. Cut out and trim your selected decoupage scraps. When cutting out the doves, cut one whole dove then cut its identical partner into elements, such as the wings and tail, which can be built up.

2 Build up the birds before they go on the birdhouse. Arrange the wings and tails onto the whole birds to check the fit, trim if necessary. Using the silicone glue, apply dots onto the whole bird and place the wings and tails into position. Don't press the motifs too hard into the glue, just rest them so that the glue will dry with height, in turn giving the wings and tails height.

3 Once the wings and tails have been glued to the bird, curl them up to make them look as if they are in motion. Arrange them around the front of the birdhouse and mark where you want them to be attached.

4 Edge the birdhouse roof and drawer with bluebells and violets, then arrange the snowdrops so that a profusion of flowers comes out from the lower edge. Glue them down firmly.

5 Finally, glue the doves down in their premarked positions.

KEEPSAKES

Boxes, in any size or shape, are perfect for
three-dimensional decoupage and look charming covered
in blooming flowers, silver paper, charms or angels.
Fans transform a photo album into a treasured keepsake.

ANGEL MEMENTOES BOX

An old shoe box becomes a special storage box for treasured letters and cards. It features a three-dimensional angel framed in a doorway, edged with a delicate gold braid.

YOU WILL NEED

- Shoe box
- Cream-colored thick paper
- Cream-colored paper doily
- Two identical angel decoupage scraps
- Scissors
- Craft knife
- Pencil
- Gold braid
- Glue and brush
- Foam tape

1 Carefully cover the box and lid with the cream paper, cutting the paper slightly oversized at all ends and then folding under the raw edges. This will give a neatly finished look to the paper. Glue the doily onto the center of the box lid and tuck under the ends at either side.

2 Take the first decoupage scrap set and cut away the background. Use a small pair of scissors for the larger areas and a sharp knife for the more intricate areas.

3 Arrange the prepared decoupage scrap on the top of the lid, mark it in its place with a pencil, remove and then glue firmly back into place.

4 Take the second decoupage set and proceed to cut out the individual elements. Carefully cut out the angel and wings separately, the doorway arch and the tiny winged heads.

5 Begin to stick these elements over their identical images already on the box, using foam tape to give them height. To get more height, simply add more layers of foam tape.

6 Edge the decoupaged picture and the rim of the lid with gold braid, securing it with a strong glue.

CROCUS PEGBOARD

This pretty pegboard is used for hanging little potpourri bags or bunches of flowers or herbs to dry. What could be a more welcome sight than one of the first flowers of spring – the crocus – used here to great effect.

YOU WILL NEED

- Small pegboard
- Blue and white acrylic paints
- Paintbrush
- Decoupage scraps of crocuses
- Silicone rubber glue
- Dimensional paint
- Scissors/craft knife
- Cutting mat

1 Wash the pegboard with watered-down paint. Apply the glue first and if the color is too vibrant, tone it down with layers of white paint.

3 Secure the crocuses into place. Put two circles of flowers in between the three pegs and then add extra flowers at either side.

2 Cut out the crocus scraps and carefully build up the pictures, in a circular motif, using tiny dots of silicone glue to give the petals height away from the base.

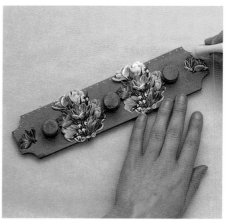

4 Add the final details by painting tiny dots of dimensional paint to frame the decoupage work and finish it off.

Upper Topa (Murree)

Haddon Hall.

SILVER HEART BOX

This heart-shaped box has been decorated with silver paper and doilies, then further embellished with pearl beads and white feathers to produce a luxurious effect.

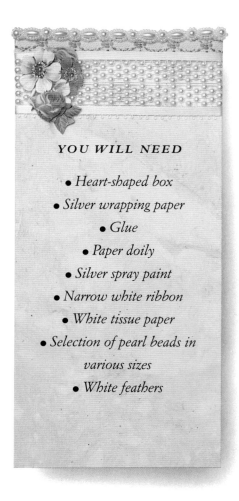

YOU WILL NEED

- *Heart-shaped box*
- *Silver wrapping paper*
- *Glue*
- *Paper doily*
- *Silver spray paint*
- *Narrow white ribbon*
- *White tissue paper*
- *Selection of pearl beads in various sizes*
- *White feathers*

1 To cover the base of the box with silver paper, cover the sides with glue and smooth the paper over, leaving an allowance at the top and bottom edges so it can be turned under. Once the sides have been covered smoothly, turn under the top and bottom edges. Spray paint a doily with silver paint and allow to dry, then cover the base of the box with it so that it overlays the silver background. To cover the lid, cut a heart from the silver paper that is slightly larger than the lid, then glue it into position. Cover the sides of the lid with narrow ribbon.

2 Cut a strip of silver paper that will fit all around the edge of the lid, covering the tabs on the sides, and glue that down into position. Cover the sides of the lid with narrow ribbon.

3 Cut a strip of white tissue paper, twist and roll it into a cord, and glue it around the edges of the heart-shaped lid, covering the silver paper join.

4 Take a large pearl bead and glue into the center of the lid, then glue smaller beads side by side around the inside of the tissue paper cord. Glue beads in rows along the diagonal of the lid. For best results, keep the beads on their strings, to keep them in place and in line as you glue. Finally, glue feathers around the large pearl bead.

FANFARE PHOTOGRAPH ALBUM

Any plain purchased photo album can be transformed with the use of some imaginative decoupage. This one is disguised with soft marbled paper and fans. The fans have been folded and flattened to give a three-dimensional effect.

YOU WILL NEED

- Photograph album
- Cream-colored marbled paper
- Transparent tape
- Cream lining paper
- Crocheted lace
- Gold braid
- PVA or white glue
- Cutting mat
- Decoupage "fan" scraps, two of each image
- Fine cream satin ribbon
- Tiny cream satin ribbon rose

1 Cover the front and back covers of the album with the cream marbled paper. Do this as if you were backing a book. Use transparent tape to tape it down, leaving the spine bare. Cut two pieces of cream lining paper that are slightly smaller than the inside covers, and glue them in place to cover the tape.

2 Arrange the crocheted lace on the spine of the album, making sure the whole spine is covered. Keep in position with a few dabs of glue.

3 Add a length of gold braid along the edge of the crocheted lace on the front of the spine; secure with glue.

4 Cut out two of each fan motifs. Taking one of each of the motifs, arrange them around the front cover, creating a composition that you like. Glue them down into place, carefully smoothing out any air bubbles.

5 Take the second set of fans and pleat them individually at the points where they would fold. Then, gluing the folded fans at either edge, stick them on top of their identical partners, which are already stuck down on the cover.

6 Cut two lengths of ribbon, fold them in half, and glue one at the center front and the other at the center back. These can be used as ties.

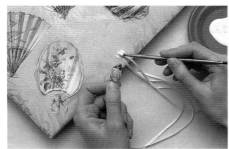

7 Finally, take the tiny satin ribbon rose and glue down at the point where the front ribbon tie is glued, to cover up the join.

OLD POSTCARDS

Scraps of flowers, doilies and lace make decorative frames for old postcards. The postcards can then be displayed to advantage on the pages of a photograph album.

YOU WILL NEED

- *Decoupage scraps of flowers,*
  borders and lace
- *Gold paper doilies*
- *Scissors or craft knife*
- *Cutting mat*
- *PVA or white glue*
- *Length of lace*

1 Cut out elements of the gold doily and the various motifs that you have chosen to frame your postcards.

2 Place the cards into position in the album and then frame the cards with decoupage scraps. Glue into place once you have decided on the composition.

3 Add posies of flowers along the edge of the page. A lace bookmark, can be glued to the inside of the book's spine.

PHOTOGRAPH ALBUM PAGES

There's no reason to stop at the cover when decorating a photo album; inside too, can have the treatment. The soft sands and grays of this paper help to enhance the cats in the photographs.

YOU WILL NEED

- *Watercolor paper and watercolor paints*
- *Paintbrushes*
- *Pinking shears*
- *Thin cardboard*
- *Pencil*
- *Sharp scissors*
- *White glue*
- *Dimensional paint*

1 Paint pieces of watercolor paper in your chosen colors using the watercolor paints. Measure your pictures for the album, and then cut the painted papers to the required measurements. Use a pair of pinking shears to make zigzagged edges. Cut oval shapes or squares from the center.

3 Use this template to make decorative edges for the framed pictures. Place the template onto the colored papers and cut the shapes to make interesting borders.

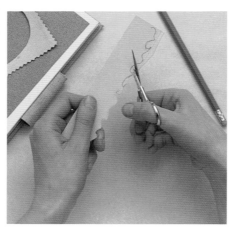

2 Make a template by drawing a wavy and curled line along a thin piece of cardboard, then cut it out carefully.

4 Place the pictures onto the page and position the frames on top. Glue them in place, then add the other decorative edges around the initial frame. Add the finishing touches with the dimensional paint.

TINY TREASURES WINDOW BOX

A small square box with a glass lid is ideal for displaying personal mementoes in a pretty way. Bits of lace and beads have been used along with angel motifs from a traditional decoupage set. However, you can use any tiny personal items to fill the box, from locks of hair to charms.

YOU WILL NEED

- Window-lidded box
- Masking tape
- Gold spray paint
- Paper doily
- Scissors
- PVA glue
- Decoupage scraps of flowers, angels and doves
- Beads
- Lace
- Foam tape
- Gold outliner paint

1 Mask off the window part of the box lid with masking tape, and spray the box with the gold paint. Shake the can well and spray at least twelve inches away from the box, in a well-ventilated area. Spray a doily at the same time.

2 Trim the doily to fit inside the window lid: cut out the center by following the scallops around the doily to create a lacy pattern.

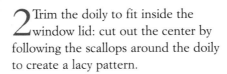

3 Fit the doily into the lid and glue face down on the glass with glue.

4 Select your decoupage images and motifs and arrange them around the base of the box. The composition should consist of the largest images at the back and the smaller ones at the front. Decide which motifs will be raised and curled as you arrange them.

5 Glue down the images that you want right at the back of the picture. Add a few beads and a sliver of lace in places where you feel they are appropriate.

6 Using foam tape, attach the other images in place. The foam tape gives height to the motifs and also allows them to be curled up at the edges. Add more layers of foam tape if you want the motifs to be higher. Stick on a few more scraps of lace and doily if you wish, making sure that the inside of the box is completely covered.

7 Place the lid onto the base and, using gold outliner paint, pipe dots all around the outside of the frame of the window lid.

SWEET CANDY JAR

This jar came with a blank lid especially designed to be decorated. The lid is decorated with simple floral decoupage scraps and finished off with gold braid and a beaded tassel. It makes a perfect gift, when filled with the recipient's favorite sweets.

YOU WILL NEED

- Round jar with decorative lid
- Decoupage flower motifs
- Scissors or craft knife
- Glue
- Foam tape
- Transparent tape
- Gold thread
- Tassel
- Beads
- Needle

1 Dismantle the lid, removing the acetate covering from the frame and the base. The metal disc from the lid will be the base of the decoupage.

2 Begin to cut flowers that will fit onto the base, and arrange into a suitable composition, layering and working out which motifs will be standing out in relief.

3 Begin gluing down the larger flowers, occasionally turning up the edges to allow other flowers to be stuck down underneath them.

4 Stick the smaller flowers down on the floral background, using foam tape so that they stand out and look three-dimensional.

5 Tape the acetate covering of the lid of the jar to the edge of the lid along the inside, so that it lies right up against the top edge. Braid two lengths of gold thread. Wind one length of it around the top edge of the lid and the other around the lower edge of the lid. Glue into place.

6 Thread the top of a tassel with a few beads and then attach the tassel to the side of the jar lid, covering the joins of the braiding. Slot the lid pieces back together and glue the base of the lid onto the frame.

CHARMING JEWELRY CHEST

This box has been simply covered in a deep red floral paper. Gold thread wound around the box, with tiny gold charms and a pretty gold clasp, create a lovely three-dimensional effect.

YOU WILL NEED

- *Small wooden chest*
- *Rose print gift wrap*
- *Ruler*
- *Pencil*
- *Scissors*
- *Glue*
- *Gold cord*
- *Glittery gold outliner paint*
- *Paintbrush*
- *Gold thread*
- *Gold angel clasp*
- *Tiny beads*
- *Tiny gold charms*

1 Measure the base and height of the chest. Add ½ inch (1 cm) all round and cut a piece of gift wrap to cover the base. Overlap the inside edges and trim the paper at the back of the box. Measure the lid, cut the gift wrap to that size and shape, adding ½ inch (1 cm) allowance. Cover the lid, overlapping the front and back. Snip tabs on the curved edges, folding the tabs over to the sides. Cut two lid sides from the paper by tracing around the sides onto the back of the paper. Cut out and glue into place, covering the tabs. Trim if necessary.

2 Cut a length of gold cord and glue it around the lower edge of the chest lid. Using the glittery gold outliner paint, add tiny dots at occasional spots all over the box.

3 Using a thin paintbrush, paint swirls of glue around the base of the lid, and place the thin gold thread onto the trails of glue, creating gold swirls across the box. Add more gold dots with the outliner paint if you wish.

4 Using fine gold thread, sew the tiny charms onto the box. Stitch them into place by catching the glued down thread with the needle and securing into position.

5 Glue the angel clasp into place at the front center of the box, attaching tiny beads around the angel for an added three-dimensional effect.

PRETTY PINK HEART BOX

This elaborate but easy concoction, ideal for holding special treasures, uses three-dimensional decoupage to great effect. Traditionally decoupaged roses are overlaid with other flowers finished off with tiny satin ribbon roses, puff paint detailing, and white silky cord.

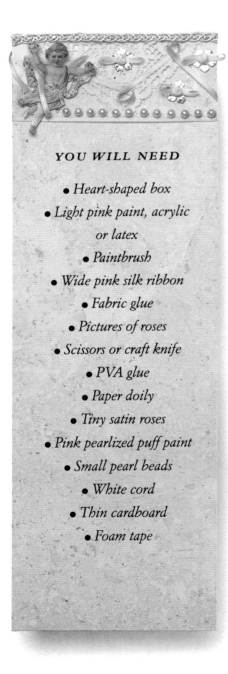

YOU WILL NEED

- *Heart-shaped box*
- *Light pink paint, acrylic or latex*
- *Paintbrush*
- *Wide pink silk ribbon*
- *Fabric glue*
- *Pictures of roses*
- *Scissors or craft knife*
- *PVA glue*
- *Paper doily*
- *Tiny satin roses*
- *Pink pearlized puff paint*
- *Small pearl beads*
- *White cord*
- *Thin cardboard*
- *Foam tape*

1 Paint the box with light pink paint, applying two coats and allowing the first coat to dry before applying the next. Cut a length of ribbon slightly longer than the circumference of the box and glue it onto the sides of the box base, gathering it slightly as you glue it down.

2 Cut out a variety of pink roses from catalogs and seed packets. Use a craft knife for the more detailed ones. Arrange these pictures on the top of the lid and glue them into position, smoothing out any air bubbles. Brush with PVA glue.

3 Cut semicircles from the doily, and glue them down around the sides of the lid to give it a lacy effect. Glue the tiny satin satin roses and paint tiny dots of pink puff paint around the lid rim.

4 Glue down pearl beads onto the top of the lid around the inside edge. Paint tiny dots of pink puff paint in between each pearl bead.

5 Select a length of white silky cord to cover the join between the edge of the decoupage and the doily sides. Glue it into position.

6 Select some small flowery motifs and glue them firmly onto a thin sheet of cardboard, then carefully cut them out. Using foam tape, attach the flowers to the lid, overlapping them and making them look three-dimensional.

TEMPLATES

Use the templates on these pages for the projects. To copy the templates, first trace the shape on tracing paper, using a soft pencil. Turn the tracing paper over and go over the outline again. Finally, position the outline onto the paper from which you will be cutting the shape. Hold it firmly in place and once more draw over the outline. For a more permanent template, transfer the outline onto cardboard.

Fold line

LACY HAND-CRAFTED ENVELOPES
page 24

HEARTS AND STARS GIFT TAGS
page 26

Rosebud gift-wrapped box
page 32

VENETIAN NEW YEAR'S EVE MASK
page 46

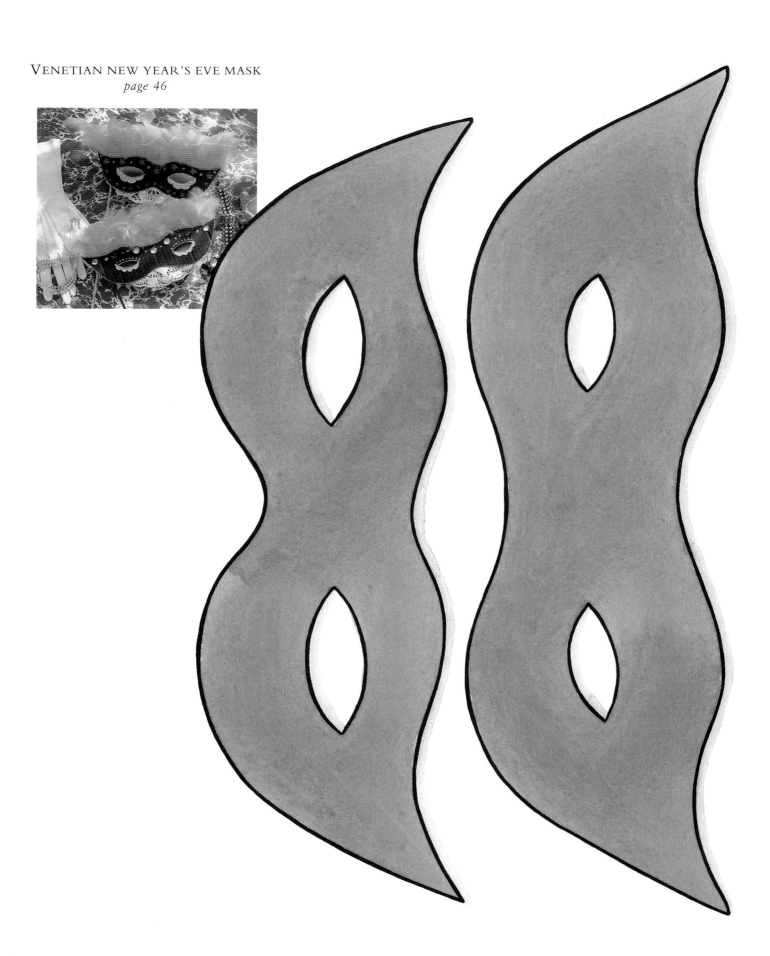

BUTTERFLY SHELF EDGING
page 72

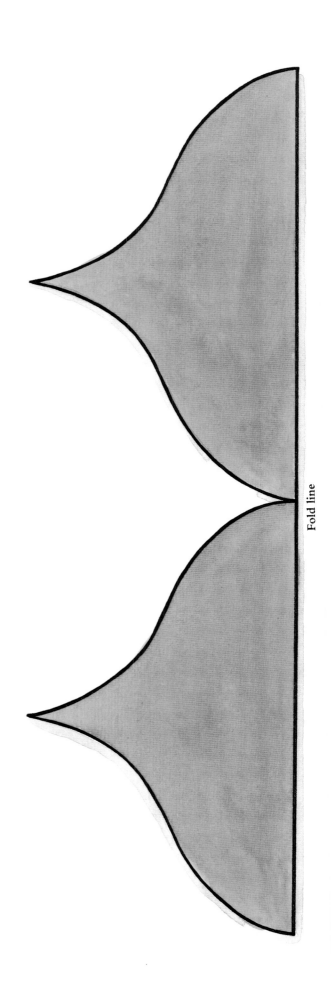

Fold line

PHOTOGRAPH ALBUM PAGES
page 94

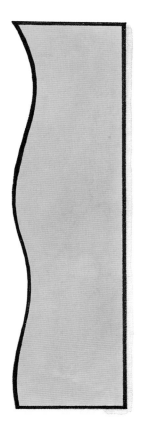

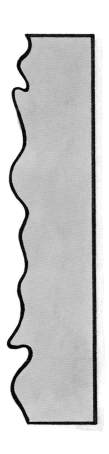
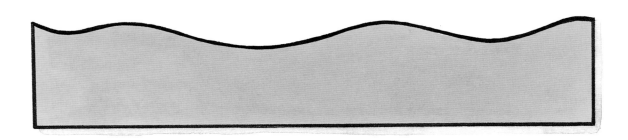
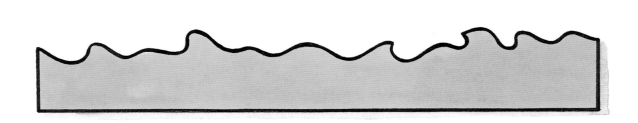

INDEX

CREDITS

The author dedicates this book to Magli Rifflard and would like to thank Creative Bead Craft, Mamelok Press Limited, and C. M. Offray and Lion ribbon for supplying material for the projects in this book.

Scraps supplied courtesy of Mamelok Press Limited, Northern Way, Bury St Edmunds, Suffolk, IP32 6NJ.

Ivory doilies kindly supplied by Artifacts, Inc., Victorian Images Division, P.O. Box 3399, Palestine, Tx. 75802. (903) 729-4178, fx. (903) 723-3903. E-Mail Artifacts @ E-Tex. com

Picture credits
6a Sally Burton; 8b Courtesy of Sheila Sawyer Decoupage Centre, Whitby, N. Yorkshire, England; 9 Andrea Wallace-Vest, courtesy of the Donald Art Company, Longwood, Florida and P.O. Box 7, Ellesmere, Shropshire, England; 10a Melanie Barnes; 11a Maxine Pharoah.

All other photographs are the copyright of Quarto Publishing Inc.

Quarto Publishing Inc would like to thank The London Graphic Centre, Sheldon Street, London WC2, for kindly loaning them materials for use in photography.

Paper tole pansy designed and illustrated by Elisabeth Dowle.

Index by Kate Robinson